First Facts®

Spotlight on the Continents

SPOTLIGHT ON

SOUTH AMERICA

by Karen Bush Gibson

CAPSTONE PRESS
a capstone imprint

First Facts is published by Capstone Press,
151 Good Counsel Drive, P.O. Box 669, Mankato, Minnesota 56002.
www.capstonepub.com

Library of Congress Cataloging-in-Publication Data
Gibson, Karen Bush.
  Spotlight on South America / by Karen Bush Gibson.
    p. cm.—(First facts. Spotlight on the continents)
  Summary: "An introduction to South America including climate, landforms, plants,
animals, and people"—Provided by publisher.
  Includes bibliographical references and index.
  ISBN 978-1-4296-6622-0 (library binding)
  1. South America—Juvenile literature. I. Title. II. Series.
  F2208.5.G536 2011
  980—dc22   2010037113

Editorial Credits
Lori Shores, editor; Gene Bentdahl, designer; Laura Manthe, production specialist

Photo Credits
Alamy/Photoshot Holdings Ltd, 21; Robert Fried, 16
Brand X Pictures, 15
Corel, 15
DigitalVision, 15
Dreamstime/Vera Volkova, 9
Photodisc, 1
Shutterstock/Daniel Wiedemann, 18; Dr. Morley Read, 13; Eduardo Rivero, 12;
    LaiQuocAnh, 9; Michael Hieber, cover; P.Zonzel, 9; thoron, 19

Artistic Effects
Shutterstock/seed

Essential content terms are **bold** and are defined at the bottom of the page
where they first appear.

Printed in the United States of America in Melrose Park, Illinois.
092010   005935LKS11

TABLE OF CONTENTS

CONTINENTS OF THE WORLD

ARCTIC OCEAN

ASIA

NORTH AMERICA

EUROPE

ASIA

ATLANTIC OCEAN

PACIFIC OCEAN

AFRICA

EQUATOR

SOUTH AMERICA

INDIAN OCEAN

N
W E
S

AUSTRALIA

SOUTHERN   OCEAN

ANTARCTICA

SOUTH AMERICA

From cities and villages to deserts and **rain forests**, variety is everywhere in South America. This **continent** has some of the world's wettest and driest areas. Rain forests get rain almost every day. Some desert areas have never had rain.

rain forest—a thick forest where a great deal of rain falls
continent—one of Earth's seven large landmasses

FAST FACTS ABOUT
SOUTH AMERICA

🌐 **Size:** 6,887,000 square miles (17,837,248 square kilometers)

🌐 **Number of countries:** 12

🌐 **Largest cities:** São Paulo, Brazil; Buenos Aires, Argentina; Lima, Peru

🌐 **Highest point:** Aconcagua, 22,834 feet (6,960 meters) tall

🌐 **Lowest point:** Valdés Peninsula, 131 feet (40 meters) below sea level

🌐 **Longest river:** Amazon river, about 4,000 miles (6,437 kilometers) long

COUNTRIES OF SOUTH AMERICA

NORTH AMERICA

CARIBBEAN SEA

VENEZUELA

GUYANA

SURINAME

FRENCH GUIANA (FRANCE)

COLOMBIA

GALAPAGOS ISLANDS (ECUADOR)

ECUADOR

BRAZIL

PERU

PACIFIC OCEAN

BOLIVIA

PARAGUAY

CHILE

Kilometers
0   500   1000
0   620
Miles

URUGUAY

ARGENTINA

ATLANTIC OCEAN

N
W   E
S

FALKLAND ISLANDS (UNITED KINGDOM)

SOUTH GEORGIA (UNITED KINGDOM)

CLIMATE

South America is known for the hot, wet **climate** of its rain forests. But many climates make up the rest of South America. Dry grasslands border the rain forests. A hot desert lies along South America's western coast. Temperatures in the mountains hardly ever rise above freezing.

climate—the usual weather that occurs in a place

LANDFORMS OF SOUTH AMERICA

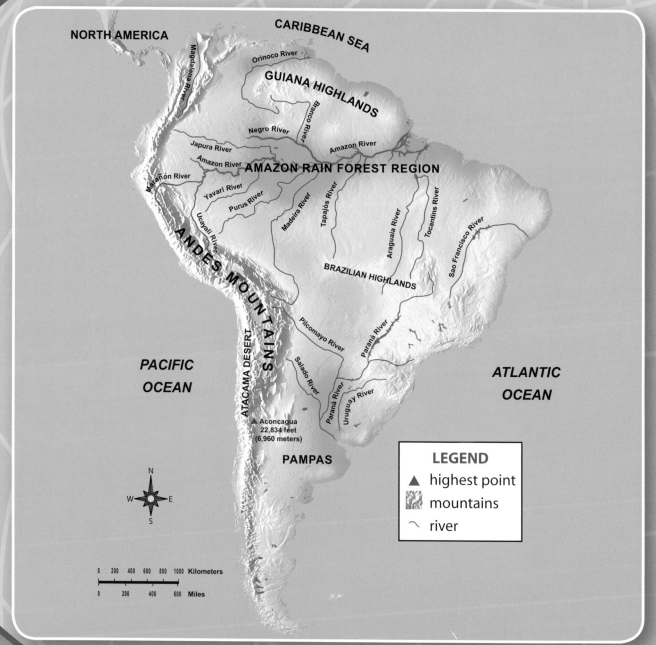

NORTH AMERICA

CARIBBEAN SEA

Magdalena River

Orinoco River

GUIANA HIGHLANDS

Negro River

Branco River

Japura River

Amazon River

Amazon River

Marañón River

AMAZON RAIN FOREST REGION

Yavari River

Purus River

Madeira River

Tapajós River

Araguaia River

Tocantins River

São Francisco River

Ucayali River

ANDES MOUNTAINS

BRAZILIAN HIGHLANDS

Pilcomayo River

Paraná River

ATACAMA DESERT

PACIFIC OCEAN

Salado River

Paraná River

Uruguay River

ATLANTIC OCEAN

▲ Aconcagua
22,834 feet
(6,960 meters)

PAMPAS

LEGEND
▲ highest point
▨ mountains
〜 river

N
W E
S

| 0 | 200 | 400 | 600 | 800 | 1000 | Kilometers |

| 0 | 200 | 400 | 600 | Miles |

LANDFORMS

South America's Andes are the world's longest mountain range above sea level. Many rivers start in the Andes. These rivers form the world's largest river, the Amazon.

The southern half of South America is covered in **plains**. The continent's driest area, the Atacama Desert, is northwest of these plains.

> **plain**—a large, flat area of land with few trees

PLANTS

Tall trees, colorful orchids, and thousands of other plants grow in the rain forest. Near the rain forest, farmers grow coffee and **cacao**. But few plants grow in the desert and mountains. Grass, cactuses, and other tough plants grow there.

cacao—a tree that produces a seed from which cocoa and chocolate are made

ANIMALS

Many animals make their homes in South America. Colorful birds, giant snakes, and billions of insects live in rain forests. On grasslands, jaguars hunt deer and other wild animals. Flightless birds called rheas munch on plants. The cold mountains are home to alpacas and llamas. Their thick fur keeps them warm.

POPULATION DENSITY OF SOUTH AMERICA

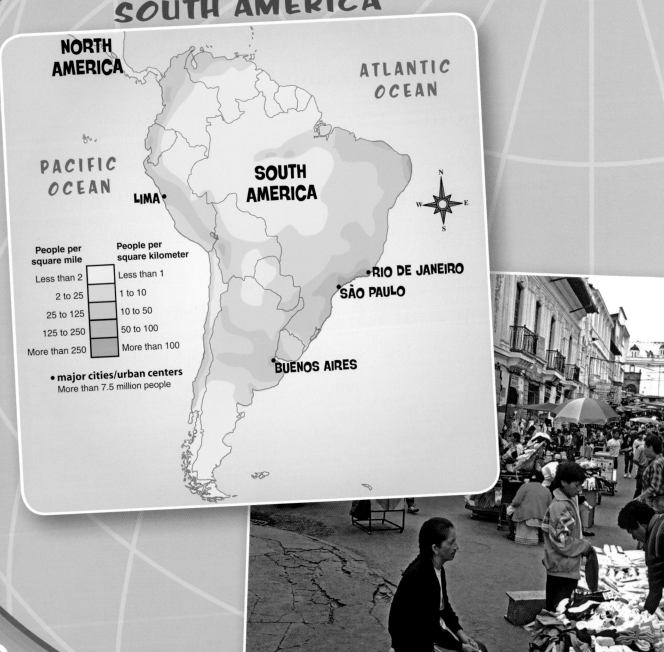

NORTH AMERICA

ATLANTIC OCEAN

PACIFIC OCEAN

SOUTH AMERICA

LIMA

RIO DE JANEIRO

SÃO PAULO

BUENOS AIRES

People per square mile	People per square kilometer
Less than 2	Less than 1
2 to 25	1 to 10
25 to 125	10 to 50
125 to 250	50 to 100
More than 250	More than 100

• major cities/urban centers
More than 7.5 million people

PEOPLE

About 396 million people call South America home. Most people live in cities along the coasts. Others live in small villages and farms.

Hundreds of languages are spoken in South America. Spanish is the main language in most countries. Millions of people also speak Portuguese.

LIVING IN SOUTH AMERICA

South America's wealthy and poor have very different lives. Wealthy people live in large houses. But millions of poor people live in **slums**. People make homes with cardboard and metal scraps in these areas.

In South America, beef, beans, and fruit are part of most meals. Coffee is also a common drink.

slum—an overcrowded, poor, and run-down area of housing in a town or city

SOUTH AMERICA AND THE WORLD

South America's Amazon rain forest is the largest in the world. It is an important world **resource**. Rain forest plants soak up harmful **carbon dioxide**. They also provide medicine and food to people. People all over the world work to protect this rain forest.

resource—something useful or valuable
carbon dioxide—a colorless gas that people and animals breathe out

GLOSSARY

cacao (kuh-KAU)—a tree that produces a seed from which cocoa and chocolate are made

carbon dioxide (KAHR-buhn dy-AHK-syd)—a colorless gas that people and animals breathe out

climate (KLY-muht)—the usual weather that occurs in a place

continent (KAHN-tuh-nuhnt)—one of Earth's seven large landmasses

plain (PLANE)—a large, flat area of land with few trees

rain forest (RAYN FOR-ist)—a thick forest where a great deal of rain falls

resource (REE-sorss)—something useful or valuable

slum (SLUHM)—an overcrowded, poor, and run-down area of housing in a town or city

READ MORE

Aloian, Molly, and Bobbie Kalman. *Explore South America.* Explore the Continents. New York: Crabtree Pub. Co., 2007.

Foster, Karen. *Atlas of South America.* World Atlases. Minneapolis: Picture Window Books, 2008.

Ganeri, Anita. *South America.* Exploring Continents. Chicago: Heinemann Library, 2007.

INTERNET SITES

FactHound offers a safe, fun way to find Internet sites related to this book. All of the sites on FactHound have been researched by our staff.

Here's all you do:

Visit *www.facthound.com*

Type in this code: 9781429666220

Super-cool stuff!

Check out projects, games and lots more at
www.capstonekids.com

INDEX